First published in Great Britain in 2018 by Search Press Limited
Wellwood, North Farm Road, Tunbridge Wells, Kent TN2 3DR

© 2016, Éditions Marie Claire-Société d'Information et de Créations (SIC)

Original French title: *J'Apprends La Teinture Pas à Pas*

English translation by Burravoe Translation Services

ISBN: 978-1-78221-555-4

The Publishers and author can accept no responsibility for any
consequences arising from the information, advice or instructions
given in this publication.

Readers are permitted to reproduce any of the items in this book for
their personal use, or for the purposes of selling for charity, free of
charge and without the prior permission of the Publishers. Any use of
the items for commercial purposes is not permitted without the prior
permission of the Publishers.

Printed in China through Asia Pacific Offset

Clémentine Lubin

★ ★ ★

A BEGINNER'S GUIDE TO DYEING & SEWING

*12 step-by-step lessons and
21 projects to get you started*

PRESS

CONTENTS

INTRODUCTION

Dyeing was off my radar for a long time. Once a year, I would redye any old pairs of trousers that were showing signs of fading. This was the extent of my relationship with dyeing – an occasional process for perking things up a bit.

One day I found an attractive bag in a second-hand shop. It was in good general shape but its colour betrayed its age. So I thought I would try dyeing it. I put it through the machine with some black dye, on the wool setting (erring on the side of caution as I didn't want to ruin it). When it came out of the machine, the colour had an uneven distribution – it was great; without meaning to, I had given it a dye effect! The bag was ready for a whole new life. I used that bag for a whole winter, which for me is a record!

Then I needed a big tablecloth for a Christmas dinner. I dyed an embroidered cotton sheet cardinal red. It was such a great success that it made the rest of my tableware look drab. I wished I'd dyed some matching napkins. So, I bought a selection of mismatched napkins at jumble sales. And... well I'm sure you get the picture.

Recently, a friend plonked a pile of lace placemats and dresses that had belonged to her grandmother in front of me and said, 'There, you'll know what to do with them!' To tell the truth, I hadn't got the faintest idea what one could do with a load of old lace placemats... but then it came to me: I could dye them all different colours!

In short, what I have learned is that dyeing is a paean to colour, and we could all do with a bit of colour in our lives! So try dyeing to get a new look, to make things more colourful and to unleash your creative spirit...

WHY DYE?

There are lots of reasons for dyeing fabric:

Refreshing
It is an excellent way of perking up the colour of clothes that have faded in the sun or over time. Most clothes can be redyed to exactly the colour you want using all-in-one kits that go in the washing machine.

Updating
Stuck with some old linen that is perfectly serviceable, but hardly used, and you don't know what to do with it? The same with those old, mismatched napkins, some of which are too worn. Dye the lot of them! Et voilà... a modern, one-of-a-kind set of table linen. Experiment with different colour dyes. Take a chance – transforming a boring old sheet into a colourful, attractive tablecloth takes no time at all.

Transforming
What can you do with that old embroidered linen, those little placemats and large, lacy tablecloths? Once again, inject them with a bit of colour. Don't hold back, but give them a second lease of life. Dyeing can transform curtains, rugs and pillows.

Personalising
It is a shame to get rid of clothing or accessories just because they are a bit worn – upcycle and dye them instead! Jeans can be made into a cheap-as-chips bag, or an old T-shirt can become your T-shirt of the summer.

This book gives you a series of step-by-step lessons teaching you all about different dyeing techniques. Then there are 21 carefully explained projects to give you some ideas!

WHAT TO DYE

Fabrics

It is easy to dye natural fibres – cotton, silk and linen – and viscose. Dyeing works less well with synthetic or new materials; the dye will not take as well. Sometimes when you dye garments you will see that the stitching remains white – this is because synthetic thread has been used.

I have had excellent results with old fabrics; cotton embroidery, embroidered monograms, lace napkins and tablecloths all take dye very well. Such items are generally made of cotton, linen, or sometimes a mixture of the two known as a linen blend. They are easy to find in second-hand shops, jumble sales or on the internet. The fabric is often of a very good quality and nice and thick. It is always worth taking a really good look before you buy, however; always unfold sheets and check the middle is not too worn, for example. If they are damaged, it is worth haggling and then you can cut them up and just use the bits that are still in good condition.

Another option is to bulk buy several metres of white cotton. Cotton comes in very broad widths and can often be a bargain. You can use it to make inexpensive curtains or bed covers. Very thick cottons, or white denim, dyed and left unironed give an interesting, crumpled effect that looks like paper.

Some fabrics are a mixture of cotton and polyester known as polycotton. You can try dyeing it but the presence of the polyester generally means the colour will not be so strong.

In this book, I have made many of the projects with a crumpled linen, which absorbs dye very well. I have also dyed clothes made of white cotton. Sometimes seams are stitched with polyester thread (often in T-shirts for example), which will stay white after dyeing.

THE QUALITIES OF DYED FABRICS

Once the dyeing process is complete, the shade may differ slightly from the colour shown on the box. This may be a result of factors other than those related to the dyeing process itself (such as soaking time and dye quantity), including:

- The base colour of the fabric.
- The composition of the fabric.

In the picture to the left, the fabric samples have all been dyed in the washing machine at 40°C (104°F) in the same dye bath. The quantity of dye and soaking time are identical.

There seem to be multiple shades. While they are all petrol blue, the intensity of the colour varies. This is mainly due to the composition and the thickness of the fabric. Thick fabrics made of pure cotton give the greatest colour and intensity.

A selection of dye samples, all dyed using the same petrol blue dye.

It can be fun to dye textured fabrics, as this often creates particular effects:

- On seersucker, the 'waffle' effect is enhanced by dyeing.

- The shiny patterns and matt background of damask fabric don't absorb the dye in the same way.

- Chambray is made up of a dark-coloured warp and a lighter weft. These threads won't take the dye in the same way.

- The thick threads of pique cotton take dye very well.

There are many different ways of weaving fabric and each fabric type will react slightly differently to the dye.

Printed cottons

You can dye printed cotton. The darker patterns will still be visible through the new dye colour. You can then create projects that combine dyed printed cotton with undyed printed cotton for a fun effect.

The base colour of your fabric

Colours given by manufacturers always assume you are going to be dyeing white fabric. There is nothing to stop you dyeing coloured fabrics, but of course you will have to dye them to a darker colour than they already are. If you dye a blue fabric red, you will get purple! The basic principle of dyeing is that your starter fabric should be lighter than the colour you want to achieve. You can't go from a dark blue to a pink, for example – the fabric would turn purple.

If a colour is too intense after the dyeing process, you can wash it again on the hottest cycle using a colour-removal product. You can also redye the fabric, adding a sandy shade. When I'm not happy with a colour, I do not hesitate: I just redye it grey or black.

Washing and maintaining dyed fabric

If you have followed the instructions for washing and rinsing your fabric, you should not have any problems at a later stage. If you have dyed a fabric at 40°C (104°F), it will be fine to put it through a wash cycle at 30°C (86°F).

Just to be on the safe side, as with all coloured fabrics, it might be wise to add a colour collector sheet to your wash. These sheets are a great invention in my opinion and since I started using them I have not had a single disaster!

All the same, it is always best to sort your laundry before putting it through the wash: put whites with whites, using a specialist laundry product that contains a whitener; the red/orange/yellow range go in a second wash, and other dark colours in a third using a biological washing product that does not attack colours.

DIFFERENT TYPES OF DYE

I have chosen to use only chemical dyes in this book. There are some great internet sites and books all about natural dyes. However, modern habits mean that most of us are unlikely to embrace dye vats (for the traditional indigo) or long processes that use mordant fixing agents. For that you would need a garden, time, plenty of patience... and the soul of a chemist! In days gone by, dyeing was an art. Each craftsman and each region had their colour of choice, which depended on the plants that grew there; from pastels to vibrant reds and everything in between.

There are lots of different sorts of dyes these days: liquid dyes, powder dyes, wool dyes, polyester dyes. The dyes are pretty much all the same. It is the form in which they are supplied that differs (liquid or powder) and whether or not the fixer and the salt are already mixed in the kit. You should always wear gloves when handling any kind of dye. You can buy dyes in pharmacies, craft shops, DIY stores and supermarkets.

Liquid dye
Consists of a pot of liquid dye and a pot of fixer. You need to add salt because it is a reactive product. I use it for hand-dyes and machine-dyes.

Powder dye
Likewise just as good for dyeing by hand or in the machine. It is more suited to smaller quantities or for adding a shade. You can seal the packet again afterwards with sticky tape. The powder is often already mixed with the fixer. You will also need to add salt.

All-in-one dye
Very practical as all you have to do is open the packet and put it in the washing machine with the clothes. Dye, fixer and salt are already mixed together.

Wool, silk and polyamide dye
These are often in powder form.

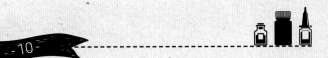

Wool, like all natural products, can be dyed, but only by hand, because wool tends to felt if it:

★ Is subject to thermal shock (you need to increase the water temperature gradually).

★ Is rubbed too hard (wool must be treated gently).

THE COLOURS

Dyeing: a paean to colour

You will be spoilt for choice.

You can dye with 'classic' colours like blue, red and black, which are all practical colours for redyeing clothes.

There are also some very nice pre-prepared mixtures available. They are very handy and in my opinion give more subtle, delicate colours. I have used them a lot in this book.

You can also make up your own mixtures. I would recommend that you use powder dyes for this to start with. Make up a small mixture. Note down the proportions you have used. Add some very hot water. Dip a chopstick in the mixture. Lay it on some absorbent white paper and wait a quarter of an hour. This will give you the shade but not the intensity, which will depend on the proportions of dye, water and fabric.

Start by dyeing a less intense colour. Then increase the quantity of dye and the soaking time of the fabric.

Dye mixing rules follow the same principles as any colour mixing:

- ★ blue + yellow = green
- ★ blue + red = purple or maroon, depending on proportions
- ★ red + yellow = orange

After this you can start experimenting with more subtle mixes:

- ★ fuchsia + red = raspberry
- ★ fuchsia + yellow = salmon pink
- ★ lilac + royal blue = lavender
- ★ aniseed green + royal blue = olive green

Note that you must never mix three colours together! You will get a sort of brownish colour.

The intensity of the colour obtained will depend on various factors:

- ★ The colour of the base fabric.
- ★ The quantity of dye in proportion to the weight of the material.
- ★ The length of time the fabric is immersed in the dye bath.
- ★ The acidity of the water (pH).

I have found that I can get a much stronger colour on fabrics dyed in the machine than I can dyeing by hand. My explanation for this is that the dyeing time is equal to a 140-minute washing machine cycle at 40°C (104°F), i.e. the water is kept hot for more than 2 hours.

I have also noticed that fabrics dyed with a red base come out of the machine much pinker than on the sample, almost certainly because of the acidity of my water. This is easy to rectify: if you are making a mixture that uses red or pink, just reduce the quantity of these two colours very slightly.

DYEING:
GENERAL PRINCIPLES

There are no two ways about it, it is essential that you wash the fabric you are going to dye first.

We have all tried it thinking, 'this material looks perfectly clean to me'. I have been tempted when I'm short of time, but it is really not a good shortcut. Stains are tricky customers – they are often hidden and only reappear during the dyeing process. The worst culprits are greasy stains, which are pretty well impossible to budge.

If the fabric is new, it has probably been treated with a stiffening primer (that white powder that you can sometimes feel on your hands). This can prevent the dye from penetrating the fibres correctly. The main difference between painting and dyeing is that dye actually penetrates the fabric.

For dyeing you need:
★ some clean fabric made of natural fibres
★ dye (liquid or powder)
★ fixer (sold with the dye)
★ table salt
★ water

You can dye in the washing machine, by hand or in the microwave (see the relevant chapters).

The intensity of the colour will depend on the proportions of the amount of fabric, the amount of dye and the amount of water.

If you are worried that the colour will be too strong, only use half the dye the first time. Repeat the process with the second half if you want a more intense colour. It is always easier to dye from lighter to darker.

If you want to adjust the colour slightly, for example if it is too bright, redye it in grey (something I did for the whole of my table linen), ecru or a sandy colour.

The colour you get will depend on a number of factors:

★ The weight of the dyed fabric in proportion to the dose of dye. To calculate this you need to weigh your fabric while it is DRY and add other pieces of material if necessary.

★ The volume of water. If you are dyeing in the washing machine, you obviously cannot choose the volume of water. Some programmes consume more water than others. The more diluted the dye, the lighter the colour; conversely the less diluted the dye, the more intense the colour.

★ Acidity of the water: I found that dyes were always slightly pinker than shown on the packaging. If you are mixing several colours together, I would decrease the amount of red very slightly.

The colour is always going to appear stronger during the dyeing process.

It will get lighter when you rinse it.

And lighter again when it has been through the drying stage.

Why do I need to add salt?

Salt is essential to dyeing – it acts as a fixer. You need it to ensure the colour 'sticks' to the fabric. For machine-dyes, you need to add 500g (17¾oz) of table salt per load, whatever the quantity of fabric being dyed.

1. You need a big bowl or basin to use for the dye bath. Be careful though - dyes are toxic so you must never use the bowl for anything food-related.

2. Scales for weighing the fabric. If the bowl on top of the scales is too small, use a kitchen plate and adjust the scales to zero before you add the fabric.

EQUIPMENT

Dyeing does not require much in the way of equipment. This is what makes it so easy!

3. Powder or liquid dye, fixer (sometimes already mixed if you are using all-in-one or powder dyes).

4. Table salt.

5. Gloves.

6. And of course something to dye! (Fabric made of natural fibres.)

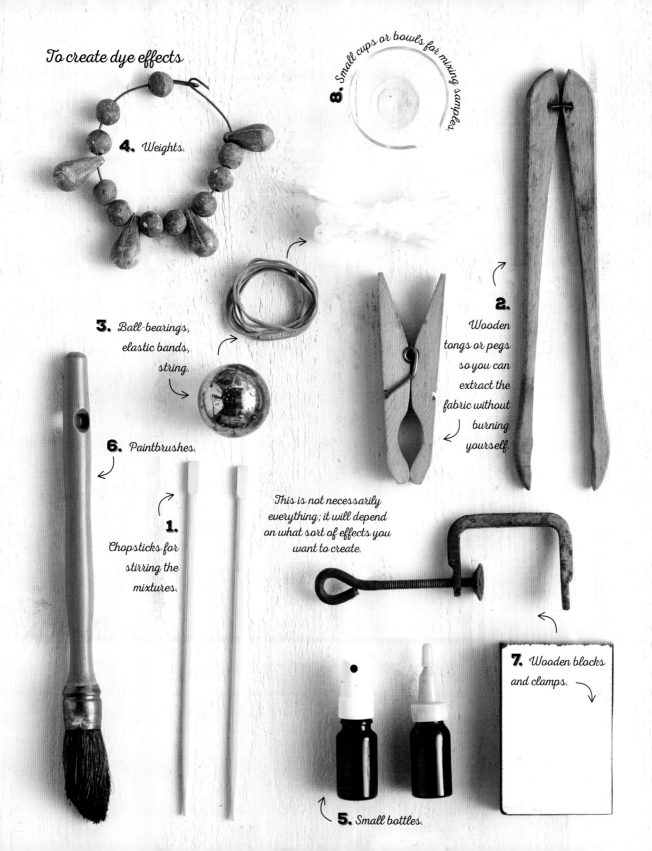

To create dye effects

4. Weights.

8. Small cups or bowls for mixing samples.

2. Wooden tongs or pegs so you can extract the fabric without burning yourself.

3. Ball-bearings, elastic bands, string.

6. Paintbrushes.

1. Chopsticks for stirring the mixtures.

This is not necessarily everything; it will depend on what sort of effects you want to create.

7. Wooden blocks and clamps.

5. Small bottles.

SEWING BOX

A well-stocked sewing box will be useful when you are crafting the projects I have suggested in this book.

A basic sewing machine is often handy: we will use straight stitch, backstitch and zigzag stitch. There is no need for any expertise, as everything will be carefully explained.

Your sewing box should contain:

1. A pair of sewing scissors – never let anyone use them for any other purpose! Mark them out with a piece of ribbon tied round the handle; they must only be used for textiles.

2. An unpicker. Unfortunately unpicking seems to go hand in hand with sewing! If you trim threads with scissors, sooner or later you are going to accidently cut the material.

3. Pins, needles and safety pins.

4. Reels of cotton to match your fabrics.

5. Ribbons and other trimmings.

6. Piping.

7. A one-metre (39in) dressmaker's tape measure.

8. Embroidery thread.

I also hang on to lots of things: old buttons, bits of ribbon, etc.

The main difficulty is finding them when you need them. I would advise sorting them into small transparent boxes or pots. It will save you a lot of time. Plus these make great decorations for a sewing corner!

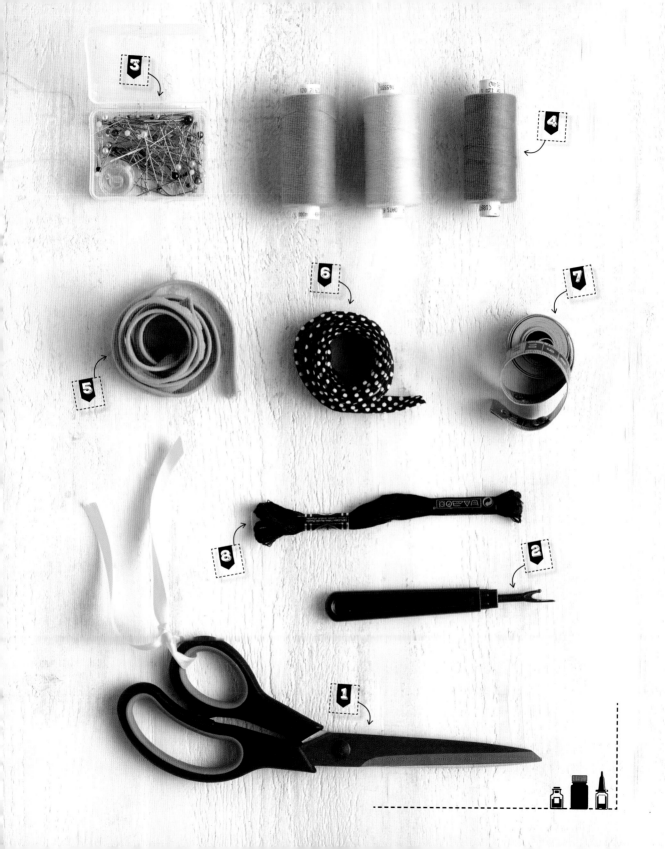

THE MAIN PRINCIPLES
of dyeing

Dyeing in the washing machine

This is the most common way of dyeing things nowadays. Dyeing in the washing machine gives a very even dye across large pieces of fabric. Here is how you do it:

1. Weigh the dry fabric.

2. Soak the pre-washed fabric in cold water.

3. Even when you are machine dyeing, make sure you put on gloves and an apron. Dye stains, but by definition it dyes – you do not want to risk spoiling your clothes. If you do get splashed, rinse immediately in hot water for as long as necessary.

4. Add the salt (generally 500g/17¾oz) and the fixer to the bottom of the washing machine drum. If you are using powder dye, open the container and pour the dye in on top of the salt.

If it is liquid dye in a pot, open the pot and put it on top of the salt. You don't even have to empty it out! Put the wet fabric into the drum and quickly start the washing machine on a long, 40°C (104°F) cycle. Some dyes, such as all-in-ones, may be more suited to a 30°C (86°F) cycle. This is the most difficult bit for me – you have to wait several hours!

5. When the dye cycle has finished, open the door and clean round the washing machine's rubber seal with some kitchen roll. This will ensure there is no dye residue lurking inside its folds. Now take a look at your fabric. Or should I say, admire it!

If necessary, take out the empty containers and run another wash cycle. Keep the wash temperature the same and add a bit of detergent, preferably biological (as it is less aggressive with the colour).

6. Run another cycle with the machine empty. This will wash the machine. Just to be on the safe side I then normally run another very short cycle with some dishcloths.

7. Allow the fabric to dry in the sun if you have a garden, or next to the radiator if you are a city-dweller. The colour becomes lighter as it dries.

Good sense dictates that you will subsequently wash dark colours together, if possible in batches of matching shades. If I have dyed fabric blue, I then wash it with my darks. I add a colour collector sheet to be on the safe side, but I have honestly never had any accidents.

Dyeing by hand

Hand dyeing is more suited to dye effects and small quantities of textiles, but it can genuinely transform a fabric. Here is how you do it:

1. Weigh the dry fabric.

2. Soak the pre-washed fabric in cold water.

3. While wearing your gloves and an apron, prepare the dye bath (dye + fixer + salt).

4. Add some very hot water: 2–3 litres (68–102 US fl oz) if you are only dyeing a small amount, up to 7 litres (237 US fl oz) for larger quantities.

5. Submerge the fabric in the dye bath.

6. Stir for a long time with a wooden stick or tongs. Using wood means you will not burn yourself.

7. Leave the fabric in the hot water for 10 to 15 minutes. You can use weights to make sure the bath covers the fabric. Stir frequently.

8. Rinse repeatedly until the water runs clear, then leave the fabric to dry.

Dyeing in the microwave

This dyeing method is very fast and great fun. It is particularly suited to small amounts of fabric. All the same, make sure you do not burn yourself. Here is how you do it:

1. Soak the pre-washed fabric in cold water.

2. Put on gloves and an apron to protect yourself. Prepare the dye bath (dye + fixer).

3. Add the salt.

4. Pour in the water, around 1–3 litres (34–102 US fl oz) depending on the quantity of fabric to dye.

5. Put the fabric in the dye bath.

6. Cover the dye bath with a lid (such as a plastic microwave lid). Put in the microwave for 5 minutes on full power.

7. Take the container out of the microwave and stir.

8. Return to the microwave on full power for 4 minutes. Remove then stir again.

9. Rinse repeatedly until the water runs clear.

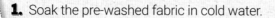

CREATING EFFECTS

Strictly speaking an offshoot of Japanese art known as 'shibori', this technique is an opportunity to have fun with dye effects.

Creating effects is a great game! There are various techniques for ensuring the dye can penetrate some areas of the fabric but not others.

You can produce these effects by hand or using the microwave, and some of them using the washing machine. Check first that the materials you are using are compatible with 1600 rpm of the washing machine.

 TIP: in any of these lessons, you can cover the areas you want to resist the dye with plastic food wrap for added protection.

LESSON 1
Creating random patterns by knotting

Knot the fabric, soak it in the dye and reveal the results. You never know what to expect!

 **1.** Roll the fabric up.

 2. Tie it in a knot. You can vary the effects by knotting it more than once; by rolling it into a ball, binding it with twine... anything goes!

 3. Soak the fabric in the dye bath. For a lighter shade, soak for a few minutes; if you want a stronger colour, leave it to soak for 10 minutes.

 4. Rinse before undoing the knot so the dye does not run onto the section that has resisted the dye. Undo the knot, rinse again and unfold.

LESSON 2
Making a big circle

You can create the effect of a sun, or a series of circles in various shades depending on soaking time.

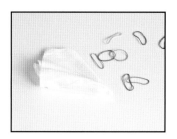

1. Find and grasp the approximate centre point of the fabric.

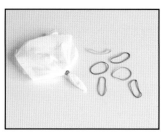

2. Wrap a rubber band or some plastic twine around the fabric. Ensure that it is very tight.

3. Add more elastic bands so the area they cover will resist the dye as much as possible. The more tightly it is wrapped, the more difficult it is for the dye to penetrate.

4. Soak the fabric in the dye bath for 15 minutes. Rinse with the elastic bands still in place. Here, the effect is even more impressive since one part of the fabric had obviously rolled itself up.

Creating a bubble effect

A classic of 1960s T-shirts, this method of creating dye resistance using beads and balls can give your fabric a lighter-than-air look.

1. Create a pleasing arrangement of the plastic balls and beads across the fabric.

2. Enclose each bead or ball in the fabric using two rubber bands.

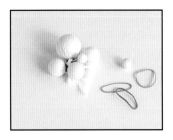

3. Attach all the balls as tightly as possible.

4. Leave the fabric to soak in the dye bath for 15 minutes, then rinse.

LESSON 4

Creating plant-like effects

Inspired by Japanese plants, such as bamboo, this method of creating areas of resistance is one of the most satisfying and attractive.

1. Wrap a strip of thick cotton fabric round a PVC tube.

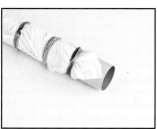

2. Secure the fabric in place using elastic bands wrapped round as tightly as possible.

3. Pucker the fabric then dip a paintbrush in the dye bath. Paint the fabric in stripes. Wait 10 minutes before rinsing.

4. By spacing out the painted stripes, you get an appealing, natural effect.

Creating a dip-dyed effect

Dip-dyeing is one of the best-known dyeing processes. This effect can transform decorative pieces like curtains and give clothes a new life.

1. Protect the part that you want to remain intact with plastic food wrap.

2. Attach the part that is not going to be dyed to a coat hanger. Soak half the fabric in the dye bath for 10 minutes.

3. Soak the bottom of the fabric for an additional 15 minutes. It will be dark, because it has remained in the dye bath for longer.

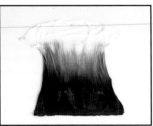

4. Create as many gradations as you want, by suspending the fabric above the dye container. For each layer, leave the fabric soaking for 5 minutes.

LESSON 6

Creating a wide, irregular line

All the poetry of Japanese dye-craft is summarised in this simplicity: like a stroke from a calligraphy brush.

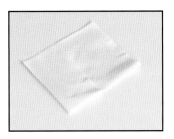

1. Fold the fabric in two widthways. Fold it very evenly the other way.

2. Hold the fabric in place with a clean clothes peg.

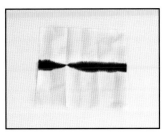

3. Soak one end of the folded fabric in the dye bath.

4. Rinse. Unfold.

Creating geometric checks

Not much work for a whole lot of effect! All it requires is a bit of geometric folding and a simple soak in the dye bath.

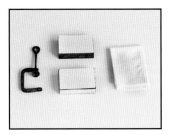

1. Fold the fabric widthways, then refold several times lengthways.

2. Insert the fabric between two wooden blocks. Hold tightly together with a clamp.

3. Soak the four ends sticking out from the wooden blocks in the dye bath.

4. Rinse, remove the wooden blocks and clamp and unfold.

LESSON 8
Creating narrow lines

More subtle and a bit trickier in terms of preparation, the narrow lines could also be curved lines, circles or geometric shapes.

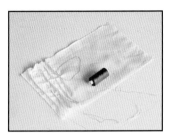

1. Draw lines onto the fabric with a textile pen. Fold the fabric along each line. Sew along the lines in straight stitch, by hand or on the machine.

2. Gather the fabric by pulling on the ends of the threads.

3. Soak the fabric in the dye bath.

4. Rinse and then pull out the threads. Unfold.

Creating effects with a spray

This method gives your projects a light and airy look. You can also roll the fabric into a ball to make areas where the dye cannot penetrate.

1. Mix a bit of dye, some fixer and some salt in a small container.

2. Use a small plastic funnel, or make one out of paper, so you can fill a bottle. Pour your mixture and some boiling water into the small glass bottle.

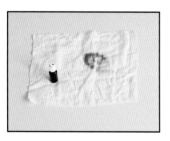

3. Spray with the bottle close to the fabric for an intense effect.

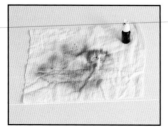

4. Spray from further away if you want a softer, more diffuse effect.

Creating a droplet effect

This effect is inspired by the works of Jackson Pollock from the 1940s. Dripping the dye onto the fabric is great fun!

1. Mix a bit of dye, some fixer and some salt in a small container.

2. Make sure you put something absorbent underneath the fabric and protect the surrounding area.

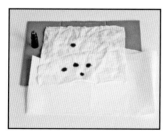

3. Use a pipette to make the droplets.

4. You can also spatter drops, Pollock-style.

Creating a 'stain' effect

Inspired by the dip-dyed paper method where you lay paper on top of colour in a pan, stain effects can completely change the look of a fabric.

1. Mix a bit of dye, some fixer and some salt in a small container.

2. Soak the fabric in a dye bath.

3. Add the first mixture to the dye bath without stirring.

4. Rinse, keeping the fabric flat.

Particular case: dyeing wool

There are two factors that cause wool to felt: thermal shock (soaking the wool in hot water) and rubbing. It is perfectly possible to dye wool without doing either of these.

1. Soak the wool in cold water.

2. Prepare the dye bath (dye + fixer + salt) with cold water. Soak the whole of the wool for an even dye, or just part of it if you want a variety of shades.

3. Slowly increase the temperature of the bath (it is sudden thermal shock that you are seeking to avoid).

4. Rinse, taking care not to let any dye run onto the undyed parts.

DYEING
in the washing machine

CROCHET THROW
with lining

EQUIPMENT

- 1 round, white, crocheted tablecloth
- 4m (158in) of fancy spotted piping
- 3m (118in) of linen fabric
- Standard sewing box accessories
- Sewing machine
- Gloves

DYE

- 1 box of all-in-one dye,
  in blue-green

★ Dyeing the throw

Dye the tablecloth blue-green in the washing machine at 30°C (86°F), following the instructions on pages 20–21. If you want to, you can also dye your 3m (118in) of linen blue-green in the machine at the same time, or use 3m (118in) of cloth in a coordinating colour.

★ Sewing the throw together

Place the dyed tablecloth on the piece of linen. Offset the tablecloth so the central pattern is not centred.

If the tablecloth is larger than the linen, pin it at regular intervals then tack/baste with long stitches. Cut off the excess tablecloth.

Sew the tablecloth to the blue-green linen on the sewing machine, a few centimetres from the edge.

★ Finishing touches

To highlight the tablecloth's scalloped edge, insert the piping between the tablecloth and the fabric. Sew in place using the machine or by hand.

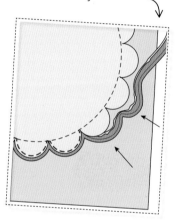

Insert the piping between the tablecloth and the fabric and sew.

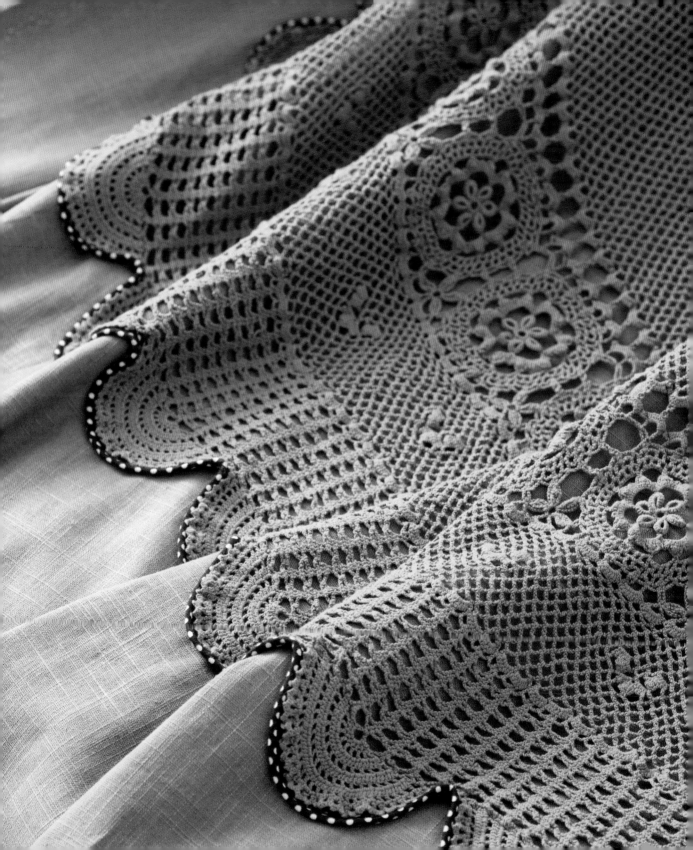

PATTERNED
pillows

EQUIPMENT

- 1 x 1.5m (39½ x 59in) white cotton fabric, or old table linen
- 6m (236in) leopard print piping
- Elastic bands
- Twine
- 2 50cm (20in) pillow pads or stuffing
- Gloves
- Ping-pong balls and small plastic balls (such as bouncy balls)
- Standard sewing box accessories
- Sewing machine

DYE

- 1 box of black dye (dye and fixer)
- 500g (17¾oz) table salt

★ Dyeing the pillows

Cut four squares of white cotton fabric, 50cm (20in) each side.

Knot ping-pong balls and plastic balls into one square using elastic bands. The more elastic bands you use, the tighter they will be and the whiter the areas they cover will come out. (Follow the instructions on page 26.)

Fold a second square in half. Roll it up. Tie some twine around it at intervals. Make sure it is tied very tightly to create areas where the dye cannot penetrate.

Dye the four squares in the washing machine, following the instructions on pages 20–21. Rinse the pieces and then the machine.

Leave to dry.

★ Sewing the pillows together

Place the piping all round a patterned dyed square, with the cord towards the centre of the square, and the raw edges aligned. Sew on the piping using your sewing machine (you may want to get a special piping foot for this job; see also right for further instruction).

Lay a second square of the plain dyed fabric on top, right sides together. Sew all round, over the original stitchline around the piping. Leave a 15cm (6in) gap in your stitching.

Clip the corners. Turn the pillow the right way out and stuff.

Sew the opening closed by hand using slipstitch.

Diagrams showing how to sew on the piping.

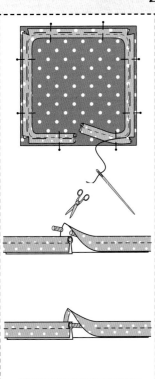

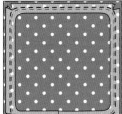

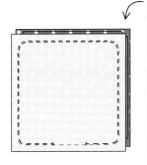

1. Lay the piping on the right side of the pillow, all the way round, with the piping cord facing inwards; notch the fabric at the corners so that it lies flat. Pin into place, then tack/baste; this keeps the piping properly in place.

2. Where the two ends meet, cut through the cord but leave an extra 1cm (½in) of material.

3. Turn the end of the upper piece under a short way. Lay it on top of the lower piece.

4. Sew on the piping using the special piping presser foot, along all the edges.

5. Place the second square of fabric on top of the first, right sides together. The piping is now between them. Sew round all sides over the initial stitchline. Leave an opening of around 15cm (6in). Clip the corners, then turn the right way out. Push out each corner. Stuff, then sew up the opening with small, invisible stitches.

PLACEMAT
tablecloth

EQUIPMENT

- 1 small single bed sheet made of linen, cotton or linen blend
- 1 set of mismatched, embroidered napkins
- 1 set of crocheted placemats, in different shapes and sizes
- Gloves

- 1 piece of flower- or leaf-pattern lace
- 1 skein of six-strand embroidery thread in pale pink
- 1 pointed embroidery needle
- Standard sewing box accessories

DYE

- 1 box of all-in-one dye, in pale pink
- 1 box of all-in-one dye, in grey

- 1 box of all-in-one dye, in indigo, for a few napkins

★ Dyeing the fabric

Dye the old sheet pale pink in the washing machine according to the instructions on pages 20–21. To get it up to the necessary weight, add a piece of lace and a few napkins and placemats.

Dye the sheet again in grey, adding some of the napkins and placemats to the load. The pink of the tablecloth will be hidden by the grey dye, but will give the grey a pinkish hue. You could simply mix the dyes and dye everything all in one go but then you would not get any pink napkins and placemats.

Dye a batch of napkins and placemats indigo. Add a linen remnant to make the vases in the next project (see page 50).

Now you have a set of three colours: grey, pink and indigo. Repeat the dyeing process as many times as you like. Add as many napkins as possible: the larger your tableware set, the more sophisticated your table will look.

Leave to dry. Iron.

★ Finishing and sewing together

Some of my napkins had monograms, so I went over them using satin stitch, sewing over the existing embroidery to make it stand out. Use a double-threaded needle.

Satin stitch

Bring the needle up through the fabric, then insert again to make a long straight stitch. Repeat further to the right and continue to form a row of stitches in this way.

Lay the dyed sheet on a table. Lay out the placemats in the centre to make a centrepiece. Arrange them attractively. You might highlight one colour against another. Pin the placemats in place. If you are using pink napkins, add a touch of matching pink to the tablecloth with a placemat, or by adding a pink embroidery motif. It is this play between the colours that makes the table so attractive.

If any of the dyed napkins are damaged, cut around the embroidery leaving a surround of 4cm (1½in). Turn under and iron to keep the fold in place.

Sew these motifs onto the tablecloth. Continue the embroidery onto the tablecloth, adding embroidered scrolls using stem stitch and touches of the cut-out embroidery (for more detail, see the photo on page 47).

Stem stitch

Stem stitch is worked from top to bottom. Make one stitch, then bring the needle up in the centre of this stitch, just off to the side. Bring the thread through the fabric and repeat, bringing the needle up just off to the side of the centre of the previous stitch.

Sew the other placemats onto the tablecloth by hand. They can overlap slightly, or be placed on top of one another.

DECORATIVE
linen vases

- 1 piece of crushed linen (for each vase you will need enough fabric to cut a circle with an 8cm/3¼in diameter, and an 11 x 26cm/4½ x 10¼in rectangle)

- Some small pieces of crochet work
- Standard sewing box accessories
- 1 glass for each vase
- 1 sheet of white paper
- Gloves

DYE

- 1 box of indigo dye (dye and fixer)
- 500g (17¾oz) table salt

★ Dyeing the fabric

Dye the piece of linen and the crochet-work indigo in the washing machine, following the instructions on pages 20–21. (For this project, the linen was dyed at the same time as the table napkins and placemats in project 3.)

As these are small pieces of fabric, you can also try dyeing in the microwave (see page 23), ensuring that you mix the dye bath repeatedly.

Rinse until the water runs clear.

Leave to dry. Iron.

★ Sewing the vases together

Trace a circle with an 8cm (3¼in) diameter on the linen for each vase. Cut out the circle.

Cut a linen rectangle 11 x 26cm (4½ x 10¼in) for each vase. Fold in two, right sides together, then sew the two short ends together, 5mm (¼in) from the edge, to create a tube.

Pin the circle to one end of the tube, right sides together. Sew together by hand, 5mm (¼in) from the edge.

Fray the material at the open end of the tube to give a fringe effect.

★ Finishing touches

Turn the vase right side out. Measure one of the small pieces of crochet. Cut a hole in the vase that it is the same size, then sew the piece of crochet into the opening.

Put the glass in the vase. Slide a piece of white paper between the fabric vase and the glass to highlight the delicacy of the crochet.

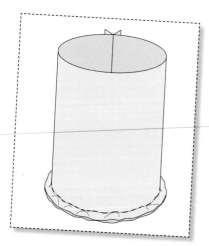

BED QUILT
with buttons

EQUIPMENT

- 1 cotton duvet cover 1.5 x 2m (59 x 79in) (or 1.5 x 4m/ 59 x 157½in) of white or natural cotton material)

- 1 piece of linen, to cover the buttons

- 4 self-cover buttons, 3cm (1¼in) in diameter

- 10 self-cover buttons of different sizes

- 1 rectangle of very thick wadding/ batting measuring 1.5 x 2m (59 x 79in)

- Standard sewing box accessories

- Sewing machine, if you are making the bed cover yourself

- Gloves

DYE

- 1 box of golden-yellow dye (the mixture contains the dye and fixer)

- 500g (17¾oz) table salt

THE PROCESS

★ Dyeing the fabric

Dye the fabric in the washing machine, following the instructions on pages 20–21. In this case, the linen fabric was dyed golden-yellow at the same time as the pillows, see page 58. You could also dye the fabric in the microwave, remembering to stir the dye bath frequently (see page 23).

★ Making the bed cover

You can use a shop-bought duvet cover, but if you want to make it yourself, cut two rectangles measuring 1.5 x 2m (59 x 79in) from the cotton fabric. Lay one on top of the other, right sides together, and stitch around one short and two long sides, 5mm (¼in) from the edge. Turn the cover right-side out.

Slip the thick wadding/batting inside the cover (whether homemade or shop-bought), making sure it is evenly distributed. Hold in place with long patchwork pins.

For homemade covers, turn the fabric in by 1cm (½in) around the open end. Stitch by hand using slip stitches.

★ Finishing touches

Cover all the buttons with the golden-yellow linen, following the manufacturer's instructions.

Sew the four big buttons in a square in the middle of the duvet cover. Make sure you sew through all three layers of fabric to keep the wadding/batting in place.

Sew the other smaller buttons randomly across the rest of the bed cover.

On this example, the location of the buttons has been chosen carefully to conceal signs of wear and tear on the cover. Covered buttons are also a good way to hide small stains.

How to cover buttons

Sew a gathering thread around the edge of your fabric circle. Lay the fabric face down and place the button upside down on top.

Pull gently on the thread and the fabric will cover the button. Knot the thread.

Clip the back of the button onto the covered front. The stitching is now hidden.

6

GOLDEN-YELLOW
crocheted pillows

EQUIPMENT

- 1.5 x 1.4m (59 x 55in) thick white linen or cotton
- 1 set of white or natural cotton crocheted placemats
- You can either make your own piping or buy it ready-made (I used both). To trim all three pillows you will need about 4.8m (189in) of piping, or the same length of coordinating fabric, bias-cut into a 3cm (1¼in) wide strip (see page 60), plus the same length of piping cord
- Gloves
- Pillow stuffing
- Standard sewing box accessories
- Sewing machine

DYE

- 1 box of golden-yellow dye (the mixture contains the dye and fixer)
- 500g (17¾oz) table salt

★ Dyeing the fabric

Using the golden-yellow dye, dye your white linen or cotton fabric and a set of crocheted placemats in the washing machine, following the instructions on pages 20–21.

Rinse. Leave to dry.

★ Preparing the rectangular pillow, made with a placemat and piping

Cut out two rectangles from the thick cotton or linen material, each measuring 25 x 50cm (10 x 20in).

Tack/baste a large placemat onto one of the rectangles, to prevent it moving about. Do not centre it; if necessary, it can overlap the edge of the linen rectangle.

Preparing the square pillow, made with a placemat and piping

Cut out two 37cm (14½in) squares from the thick cotton or linen material. Lay a placemat on the right side of one of the squares. It does not matter if it is bigger than the piece of material. Tack/baste the placemat to hold it in place.

Preparing the plain pillow, made with piping

Cut out two 37cm (14½in) squares, from the thick cotton or linen material.

The same method for sewing up the pillows is used in all three projects.

★ Preparing the piping

Piping was originally used to limit the wear on upholstered furniture, but nowadays it is used to add a touch of colour, allowing you to match the pillows to your colour scheme. You can buy it ready-made (as I used on two of the pillows, or you can make your own).

If you are making your own, bias-cut the fabric, joining the strips together to get the required length.

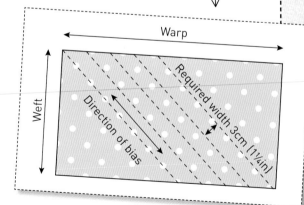

Place the cord along the centre of the fabric band, on the wrong side. Tack/baste the material over the cord. Stitch, enclosing the cord in the material.

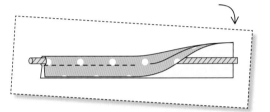

★ Sewing on the piping

For each pillow, place the piping around the edge of the right side of a fabric piece – position with the side enclosing the cord to the inside of the pillow, and put a notch in each corner to help the fabric lie flat. Pin in place, then tack/baste.

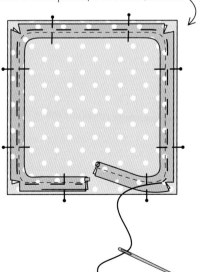

Stitch together on the sewing machine. You can use a special piping presser foot if you have one. Some sewing machines allow you to offset the needle to the left; if so, put the needle as far to the left as possible.

Lay the second piece of material on top of the first, right sides together, lining up the edges. Stitch around again, following the stitchline to attach the piping, but leave a 10cm (4in) opening.

★ Finishing touches

Cut off any excess placemat if necessary. Clip the corners of the pillow – this helps the corners stay nice and sharp.

Turn the pillow cover right side out.

Stuff the filling inside.

Turn under about 5mm (¼in) on each side of the opening. Sew closed by hand using slipstitch.

NAVY BLUE
pillowcase

7

EQUIPMENT

- 1 old cotton, linen or linen-blend Oxford pillowcase

- Gloves

DYE

- 1 box of navy blue dye (dye and fixer)

- 500g (17¾oz) table salt

★ Dyeing the pillowcase

Wash the pillowcase. You need to be careful with old pillowcases: they often look clean but it is best to run them through a 60°C (140°F) wash before dyeing them, as otherwise grease stains can appear during the dyeing process. It is advisable to leave old linen to soak for a night in water and Marseille soap (a hard French soap made from vegetable oils).

Weigh the pillowcase while it is dry. (You might need to add other items such as a pair of jeans or some offcuts of fabric to reach the weight you need for the bath.)

Dye all the fabric navy blue in the machine, following the instructions on pages 20–21.

Leave to dry.

★ Finishing touches

Iron the pillowcase.

Before ironing a pillowcase with embroidery detailing, lay a few towels on your ironing board to create a softer surface so that you do not damage the embroidery.

BOLSTER
cover

EQUIPMENT

- 1 old cotton, linen or linen-bend Oxford bolster cover

- Gloves

DYE

- 1 box of navy blue dye (dye and fixer)

- 500g (17¾oz) table salt

THE PROCESS

★ Dyeing the fabric

Wash the bolster cover. It is advisable to leave the bolster to soak in Marseille soap overnight.

Weigh the bolster cover while it is dry. Add a third less dye than needed for the weight of the fabric.

Add the navy blue dye, the fixer and the salt to the bottom of the washing machine drum. Put in the bolster cover. If it is dry, do not wet it. You are looking for an uneven dye effect here.

Set the machine to a 30°C (86°F) wool programme. The wool programme does not actually spin the fabric, it just wets it. As a result, the dye will be unevenly distributed. Rinse normally in the machine (see also pages 20–21).

★ Finishing touches

Iron the pillowcase.

Before ironing a pillowcase with embroidery detailing, lay a few towels on your ironing board to create a softer surface so that you do not damage the embroidery.

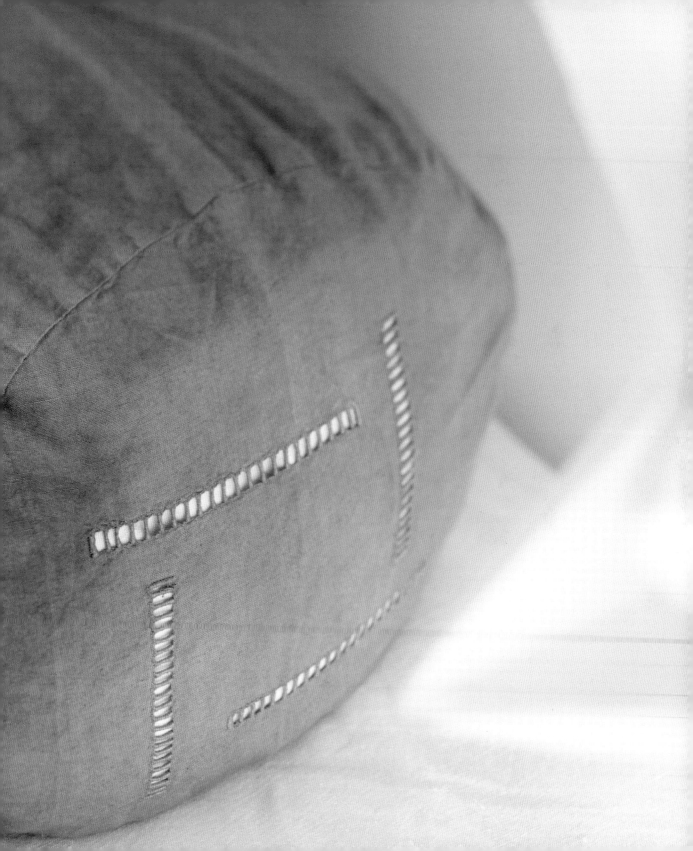

HAND TOWEL
and wash mitt

EQUIPMENT

- 1 big white hand towel, or 60 x 110cm (24 x 43½in) of white towelling
- 1 white wash mitt
- 20cm (8in) of yellow satin ribbon

- 1 bag of sturdy elastic bands
- Plastic baubles
- Ping-pong balls
- Small rubber balls
- Gloves

DYE

- 1 box of petrol blue dye (dye and fixer)

- 500g (17¾oz) table salt

THE PROCESS

★ Dyeing the fabric

Weigh the fabric while it is still dry.

Knot the baubles into the towelling using the elastic bands. Add several elastic bands to secure very tightly. Knot the ping-pong balls and then the smaller balls into the towel and the wash mitt (see the instructions on page 26 for creating a bubble effect).

Soak the pre-washed towelling.

Put a bit of salt in the bottom of the machine, open the dye and put it on top of the salt with the fixer. Pour in the rest of the salt.

Place the wet material on top and run a long cotton cycle at 40°C (104°F) (see also pages 20–21).

Remove the balls, then wash the towel and mitt in the washing machine.

Rinse out the machine.

Leave to dry.

★ Finishing touches

If you have used towelling material instead of a towel, dyeing it without hemming first will result in a bit of fraying. Trim off in a straight line to create a fringe effect, or sew a simple double hem.

Cut the satin ribbon into two 10cm (4in) lengths. Tie the ribbons to the hanging loop on the wash mitt.

 WARNING: do not put any marbles or larger snooker-type balls in the washing machine – if they become detached they could break the glass in the door.

FAUX PAPER
storage bag

EQUIPMENT

- 60cm (24in) thick white or natural linen
- 1 leather-look buckle set
- 1 reel of golden-yellow sewing thread
- 1 water-washable textile marker pen
- Standard sewing box accessories
- Sewing machine
- Gloves

DYE

- 1 box of golden-yellow dye mix (dye and fixer)
- 500g (17¾oz) table salt

THE PROCESS

★ Dyeing the fabric

Dye the fabric golden-yellow in the washing machine, following the instructions on pages 20–21.

★ Cutting the fabric

Cut a 7 x 25cm (2¾ x 10in) rectangle from the linen for the base, two 25 x 60cm (10 x 23¾in) rectangles for the front and back of the bag, and two 7 x 60cm (2¾ x 23¾in) rectangles for the sides.

★ Sewing the bag together

Place the base and the front piece right sides together, lining up the 25cm (10in) edges. Stitch together with a 5mm (¼in) seam allowance.

Assemble the base and the back, right sides together, again lining up the 25cm (10in) edges. Stitch.

Assemble the base and the sides, right sides together, lining up the 7cm (2¾in) edges. Stitch.

Stitch along the sides to complete the bag, right sides together.

Hem the top of the bag using zigzag stitch (fold over a simple double hem then secure with stitching).

Clip the corners, then turn the bag the right way out.

Sew along each edge of the bag, 3mm (⅛in) from the edge. This reinforces the seams and makes it look more like a paper bag!

To close the bag, fold the top over by 12cm (4¾in) towards the front. Fold it again, by another 12cm (4¾in).

Position the buckle in the middle of the bag. Mark its position with a water-washable textile marker pen (the bottom of the buckle strap should be around 6cm/2½in from the bottom).

Unfold the bag and machine sew the buckle into place using the golden-yellow thread.

 TIP: leave the fabric unironed to retain the crumpled effect.

11

DENIM & LEATHER
satchel bag

EQUIPMENT

- The tops of both legs of a pair of jeans (around 30cm/12in)
- 1 piece of brown leather 20 x 20cm (8 x 8in), plus a small scrap
- 1 leather over-the-shoulder strap
- Standard sewing box accessories
- Sewing machine
- 2 snap hooks
- Gloves

DYE

- 1 box of navy blue dye (dye and fixer)
- 1 box of black dye (dye and fixer)
- 1kg (35¼oz) table salt

★ Dyeing the fabric

Dye the pieces of denim in the washing machine, following the instructions on pages 20–21: dye one leg black, the other navy blue.

★ Sewing the bag together

Cut the black denim leg piece to a length of 30cm (12in). Choose which side you want to be the front, and sew the leather scrap in place, about 5cm (2in) from the bottom on either side. Turn the denim inside out, then sew the bottom edge together with a 5mm (¼in) seam allowance to create a pouch.

Clip the corners. Turn the right way out.

Turn in around 3cm (1¼in) around the top edge, then stitch.

Cut the blue denim leg piece to a length of 23cm (9in). Turn the leg inside out, then sew the bottom edge together with a 5mm (¼in) seam allowance.

Clip the corners. Turn the right way out.

Turn in around 3cm (1¼in) around the top edge, then stitch.

Lay the two pockets on top of each other. Attach together by hand sewing one side of each pocket together.

Lay the leather flap over the big black pocket, right sides facing. Sew it along the top of the pocket, i.e. along the side that is not attached to the blue pocket.

★ Preparing to attach the shoulder strap

Cut the oversewn seam from the piece of denim remnant. Cut this band into two equal lengths.

Fold them in half.

Sew both onto each side of the bag to form loops.

Attach the leather shoulder strap to the snap hooks that you will then clip to the loops.

HAND
dyeing

12

LANDSCAPE
scatter pillows

EQUIPMENT

- 1 x 1.4m (39½ x 55in) white linen
- 2 small atomiser bottles
- 2 small dropper bottles
- 2 skeins of six-strand embroidery thread in grey
- 1 sharp embroidery needle with a large eye

- Pillow stuffing
- 2.5m (98½in) of fluorescent piping per pillow
- 1 water-washable textile marker pen
- Sewing machine
- Gloves

DYE

- 1 sachet of blue dye (the fixer is already mixed with the powder)
- 1 sachet of green dye (the fixer is already mixed with the powder)

- 1 sachet of red dye (the fixer is already mixed with the powder)
- 1 sachet of purple dye (the fixer is already mixed with the powder)
- 4 teaspoons table salt

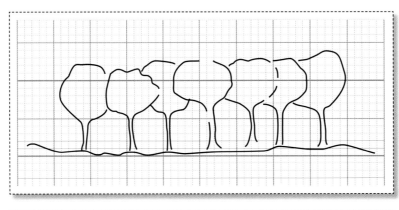

Pattern for the tree pillow
1 small square =
1cm (½in)

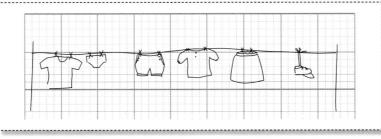

Pattern for washing line pillow
1 small square = 1cm (½in)

★ Dyeing the fabric

Cut two 50 x 60cm (20 x 24in) rectangles per pillow from white linen.

Fill the two atomiser bottles with a mixture of dye and bit of table salt: one with the blue dye, the other with the green. Add a bit of boiling water. Spray the upper half of one rectangle with the blue. Rinse and now turn upside down so the blue area is at the bottom and the undyed part remains intact. Spray the undyed part green then rinse (see page 32).

For the washing line design, spray the whole pillow front blue, then rinse. Put some red dye, green dye and purple dye in the dropper bottles, along with salt and boiling water. Drop six large drops into the centre part of the pillow. Leave to dry, then rinse, keeping the fabric flat so the dye does not run. Leave to dry.

★ Preparing the design

Copy the design of your choice, scaling it up to the right size. Attach the material onto the drawing with adhesive tape. Place against a window and trace over the design with a water-washable textile marker. Embroider over the lines in stem stitch using two strands of embroidery thread. Add details using cross stitch, stem stitch and French knots (see below for more information).

★ Sewing the pillows together

Pin the piping all round the edge of the right side of one pillow piece, with the cord towards the centre. Stitch in place on the sewing machine.

Lay the second rectangle on top of the first, right sides together, then stitch right round over the first stitchline (the piping stitchline). Leave a 15cm (6in) opening. Clip the corners. Turn the pillow the right way out. Stuff. Sew the opening closed by hand with slipstitch.

Cross stitch

Stem stitch

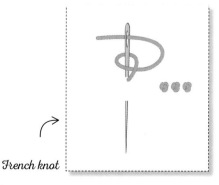

French knot

Attaching piping

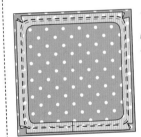

Put a notch in the piping fabric at each corner to help it lie flat. Sew on the piping using a piping foot, if you have one, around all four edges.

Lay the second square of fabric on top of the first, right sides together, with the piping between them.

Sew around over the initial stitchline. Leave an opening of around 15cm (6in), trim the corners and turn the right way out. Stuff. Push out each corner. Sew up the opening with small stitches.

TEA TOWEL
and potholder set

EQUIPMENT

- 20 x 110cm (8 x 43½in) very thick white cotton
- 3 cotton baby muslins
- 5 silver eyelets, 2.2cm ($^7/_8$in) diameter
- Standard sewing box accessories
- Sewing machine
- 1 hammer
- 1 bag of elastic bands
- 1 large paintbrush
- 1 large clothes peg or bulldog clip
- 1 plastic tube, 10cm (4in) in diameter (it does not matter if the diameter is different to this)
- 2 blocks of wood or chipboard of the same size
- 2 clamps
- Gloves

DYE

- 1 sachet of navy blue dye (the fixer is already mixed with the powder)
- 1 aniseed-green liquid dye kit
- 400g (14oz) table salt

THE PROCESS

★ Dyeing the fabric

Wash the fabric.

Make a dye bath using the navy blue dye, salt and very hot water.

★ Preparing the stripy towel

Fold a muslin into even pleats. Hold the pleats in place with a large clothes peg or bulldog clip.

Dip approximately 1cm (½in) of the folded edges of the muslin in the dye for around three minutes.

Do not unfold the muslin. Rinse thoroughly. Make sure you do not let the dye run onto the undyed part during the rinsing process.

Leave to dry.

★ Preparing the half-dyed towel

Soak half of another muslin in the dye bath for several minutes (see page 28). Rinse thoroughly ensuring that the dye does not drip onto the undyed area.

Leave to dry.

★ Preparing the checked towel

Fold a muslin into even pleats. Slide it between two wooden blocks.

Squeeze the wooden blocks together as tightly as possible with the clamps. The tighter you can get the clamps, the less the dye will penetrate.

Wet several times in the dye bath. Rinse thoroughly without removing from the wooden blocks (see page 30).

★ Finishing the towels with eyelets

Snip a hole in one corner of each muslin with a pair of scissors.

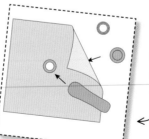

Position the male and female parts on each side. Slide into the setting kit.

Tap with small blows of the hammer.

★ Dyeing the potholders

Wrap the strip of white fabric around the plastic tube. Hold in place with elastic bands along the whole length. The tighter you can get the elastic bands, the whiter the areas underneath will remain.

Concertina the material and reduce the length of the band to a minimum.

Make an aniseed-green dye bath. Dip a paintbrush in the dye bath and paint wide brushstrokes down the puckered material (see page 27).

Rinse thoroughly. Leave to dry.

★ Making the potholders

Cut out 20cm (8in) squares. Lay them in pairs, right sides together. Stitch around three sides with a 5mm (¼in) seam. Turn the right way out. Turn in the two edges of the fourth side and secure with hand or machine stitches.

Set an eyelet in one corner.

OMBRE
T-shirt

EQUIPMENT

- 1 white, long-sleeved cotton T-shirt
- 40 x 110cm (15¾ x 43½in) white cotton voile
- Elastic bands or twine
- Plastic food wrap
- 1 skirt hanger
- Standard sewing box accessories
- Gloves

DYE

- 1 box of teal dye (dye and fixer)
- 400g (14oz) table salt

★ Dyeing the T-shirt

Dilute the dye in boiling water, then add the fixer and salt.

Soak the cotton voile. Stir evenly, then leave in the dye bath.

The T-shirt was dyed by hand using the dip-dye process to create an ombré effect (see page 28). Roll up the top of the T-shirt in plastic food wrap to protect it, then put elastic bands around it and attach it to a skirt hanger. Soak the bottom of the T-shirt and the bottom of the sleeves for 15 minutes in the dye bath.

Then allow slightly more of the T-shirt to soak for 3 minutes.

Rinse the T-shirt thoroughly, keeping the top of it well protected so that it does not get stained. Leave to dry.

Rinse out the cotton voile. Leave to dry.

★ Sewing the T-shirt together

Cut out two bands from the cotton voile, measuring 15 x 50cm (6 x 20in).

Hand sew the two short ends together, right sides facing, to create a 'loop' of fabric. Fold in two widthways, wrong sides facing in. Sew a gathering stitch with doubled thread through the long open edge opposite the fold. Gather by pulling on the threads until the circle is the diameter of the bottom of the T-shirt sleeve. Sew on, stitching through the hem at the end of the sleeve.

15

COLLAR

EQUIPMENT

- 1 vintage crocheted collar
- 1 small mother-of-pearl button
- Standard sewing box accessories
- Gloves

DYE

- 1 box of black dye (dye and fixer)
- 200g (7oz) table salt

★ Dyeing the collar

Find an attractive vintage crocheted collar. This is probably the trickiest part of this project! They are often sold in batches, which means you can select the prettiest one. Do not worry too much about what it is made of; old collars are crocheted with very strong, high-quality cotton yarn.

They are, however, often stained. Leave the collar to soak in a basin with Marseille soap overnight.

The collar is hand-dyed (although you could dye in the washing machine or the microwave).

Prepare the dye bath with the black dye, fixer, salt and boiling water. Use a bit of water to dilute very slightly. The colour is very concentrated.

Add the collar and stir evenly for a long time to ensure the dye is well distributed and the colour is even. Rinse.

★ Finishing touches

Sew a mother-of-pearl button on the opening after dyeing so it stays white.

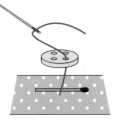

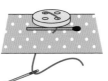

Sewing on a button

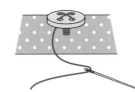

Take a length of thread, (maximum 30cm/12in in length - if it is any longer, it might get knotted). Slip a matchstick between the fabric and the button to create a shank. Bring out the thread through one of the holes in the button.

Pass it back down through another hole. Repeat several times, then sew the other two holes in the same way.

Remove the match. Wrap the thread around the 'shank' and then tie off the thread securely.

16

SPOTTY PASTEL
shirt dress

EQUIPMENT

- 2 white cotton shirts: one in your size, the other two sizes bigger
- 3 dropper bottles (1 per dye colour)
- 1 safety pin
- Gloves
- Standard sewing box accessories
- Sewing machine

DYE

- 1 sachet of green dye (the fixer is already mixed with the powder)
- 1 sachet of indigo dye (the fixer is already mixed with the powder)
- 1 sachet of orange dye (the fixer is already mixed with the powder)
- 60g (2oz) of table salt

★ Choosing the shirts

This dress is made of two white cotton shirts cut up and reassembled. Choose a shirt in your size. Buy a second identical one, two sizes bigger. To be on the safe side, pass the second shirt around your hips to make sure you can button it up without difficulty and it is not too tight.

★ Preparing the skirt of the dress

Unpick the pocket on the larger shirt. Cut the shirt off just underneath the armholes. You only need to keep the bottom part of this shirt, to make the 'skirt' of your dress.

★ Sewing the dress together

Tack/baste the cut shirt, now a skirt, onto the bottom of the shirt that has not been cut, right sides facing, making sure you align the side seams and button plackets.

Try it for length. You might need to cut off a bit of the shirt around the hips. Adjust the lengths of the two shirts until you have the look you want. Stitch together. Oversew the seam. Put the surplus fabric to one side to make the belt and belt loops.

Stitch and oversew the two shirts together.

★ Making the belt loops

Cut the button band from the unused parts of the shirts in 5cm (2in) lengths to make the belt loops. Turn under 5mm (¼in) at each end. Sew on five over the seam where the shirts meet.

★ Making the belt

Create two fabric strips, measuring 4 x 80cm (1½ x 31½in), from the leftover fabric. Place one on top of the other, right sides together. Stitch the long sides together. Turn the right way out with the help of a safety pin.

Turn in at each end. Sew closed by hand using slipstitch.

★ *Dyeing the dress*

Wash the dress

Fill each bottle with a small amount of dye and salt. Add some hot water (take care not to burn yourself). To ensure the dye is hot enough, put the bottle in the microwave for a few minutes.

Unbutton the dress and spread it out on some cardboard or some old newspapers. Lay the belt flat.

Squirt some splodges of colour onto the bottom of the dress. Dye colour by colour. Rinse thoroughly, ensuring that it stays flat and allow to dry between each colour. Some colours may run slightly during the rinsing process: let them – it adds to the effect.

17

SKY BLUE SCARF
with trim and tassels

EQUIPMENT

- 70 x 140cm (27½ x 55in) light white cotton fabric

- 1 small, glass atomiser bottle

- 4 skeins of embroidery thread: 1 each

- of pink, fuchsia, red and yellow

- 1 large, pointed embroidery needle

- 1 piece of cardboard

- Gloves

DYE

- 1 sachet of royal blue dye (the fixer is already mixed with the powder)

- 1 teaspoon of table salt

THE PROCESS

★ Dyeing the scarf

Fill the atomiser bottle with a mixture of the dye, salt and very hot water. Crumple the fabric roughly into a ball.

Spray the dye onto the fabric ball (see page 32). Crumple up again, and repeat the process.

Rinse thoroughly. Leave to dry.

★ Stitching the scarf

Do not iron the fabric. Turn over each edge twice by a few millimetres and stitch in place to make the hem.

Embroider round the edge using blanket stitch using six strands of embroidery thread. Space the stitches about 2–3mm (⅛in) apart. Change colour each time you run out of thread.

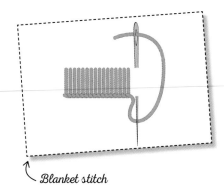

Blanket stitch

★ Making the tassels

Cut a 6cm (2½in) square of cardboard. Using the remaining embroidery thread, make four tassels as follows: wrap the thread round the cardboard. Pass a 10cm (4in) piece of thread through the middle of the loops and knot – you will use this for sewing the tassel onto the scarf. Holding the loops carefully in place, cut the thread at the bottom and remove the cardboard. Wrap another piece of thread round the top quarter to create a tassel. Make one tassel in each colour. Sew a tassel onto each corner.

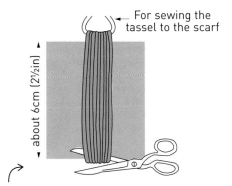

For sewing the tassel to the scarf

about 6cm (2½in)

Wrap the thread around the cardboard. Pass a piece of thread through the top of the loops. Cut through the loops at the bottom.

Tie off the top quarter of the tassel with another piece of thread.

ZIP-UP BAG
with front-facing zip

EQUIPMENT

- 35 x 140cm (14 x 55in) white cotton
- 25cm (10in) zip
- 1 water-washable textile marker pen
- 1 long ruler
- Some linen yarn
- Standard sewing box accessories
- Sewing machine
- Gloves
- Kitchen scissors
- 1 piece of cardboard

DYE

- 1 box of navy blue dye (dye and fixer)
- 200g (7oz) table salt

THE PROCESS

★ *Dyeing the fabric*

Draw some regular parallel lines, 2cm (¾in) apart on the white cotton with a water-washable textile marker pen. Fold the fabric along each line. Stitch on the machine using long stitches, 2mm (⅛in) from the fold. Gather by pulling on the threads (see page 31).

Wash the fabric.

Prepare the dye bath with the dye, fixer, salt and boiling water. Soak the fabric in this bath for around 10 minutes. Stir evenly with a wooden chopstick.

Rinse thoroughly. Pull out the gathering threads. Leave to dry. Iron.

★ *Sewing the zip-up bag together*

Cut a 20 x 35cm (8 x 14in) rectangle from the dyed fabric. Hand dyeing is not always even, so choose the area of the fabric that you like best!

1. Lay the zip right sides together along one of the 20cm (8in) sides. The zip should overhang at both ends. Stitch together on the sewing machine.

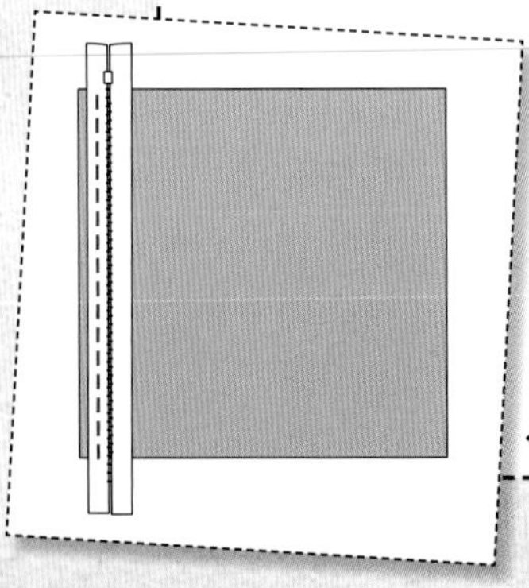

2. Fold the rectangle so the second 20cm (8in) side is right sides together with the other side of the zip. Stitch.

3. Half open the zip: this is very important. Fold the body of the bag, right sides together, positioning the zip towards you, off-centre. Sew up the sides, then oversew them.

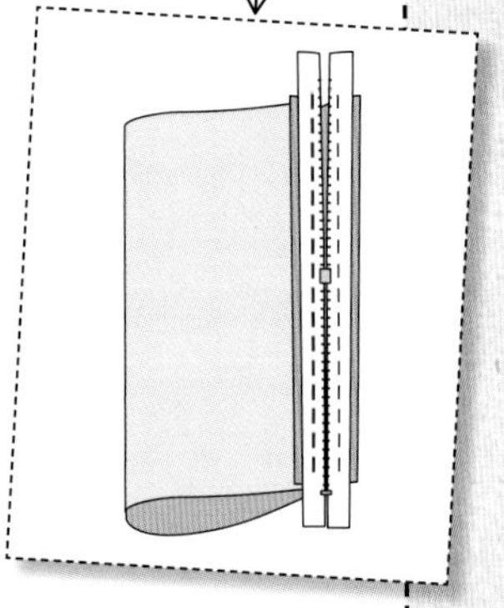

4. Cut off the ends of the zip with kitchen scissors (do not use sewing scissors, the zip could damage the blades). Turn the bag the right way out.

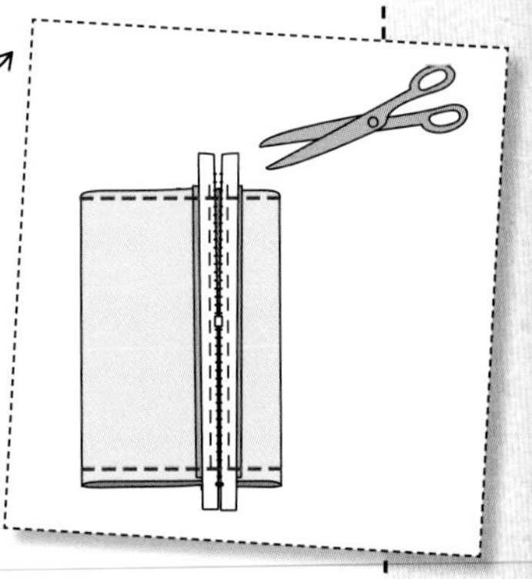

Making the tassel

Cut an 8cm (3¼in) square of cardboard and wrap the yarn around it several times. Pass a 10cm (4in) piece of yarn through the middle of the loops and knot – you will use this for attaching the tassel to the zip pull. Holding the loops carefully in place, cut the yarn at the bottom and remove the cardboard. Wrap another piece of yarn round the top quarter to create a tassel.

Knot the tassel to the zip pull.

For sewing the tassel to the zip pull

about 8cm (3¼in)

Wrap the yarn around the cardboard. Pass a piece of yarn through the top of the loops. Cut through the loops at the bottom.

Tie off the top quarter of the tassel with another piece of yarn.

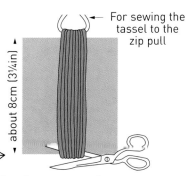

19

ZIP-UP BAG
with top zip

EQUIPMENT

- 50 x 90cm (20 x 35½in) white cotton
- 25cm (10in) dark blue zip
- Standard sewing box accessories
- Sewing machine
- 1 piece of cardboard
- Kitchen scissors
- 1 small skein of linen yarn
- Gloves

DYE

- 1 box of navy blue dye (dye and fixer)
- 200g (7oz) table salt

★ Dyeing the fabric

Wash the fabric.

Prepare a blue dye bath with the dye, fixer, salt and 1 litre (34 US fl oz) of boiling water. Do not pour in all the dye. Soak the fabric in the bath for around 10 minutes. Stir from time to time: the dye must not be too even.

Dilute the rest of the dye with a very small amount of boiling water. Pour it over the fabric in one particular place. Do not stir the dye bath. Leave it for 15 minutes.

Take out the fabric. Rinse repeatedly until the water runs clear. Leave to dry.

★ Sewing the bag together

Cut a 24 x 20cm (9½ x 8in) rectangle from the dyed fabric. Lay one 20cm (8in) side of the rectangle along the zip fastener, right sides together. Stitch.

Fold the fabric and place the other 20cm (8in) side of the rectangle against the other side of the zip. Stitch. Open the zip halfway. Stitch the two sides together then oversew. Clip the corners.

Make a 'stop' at each end of the zip fastener by oversewing over the teeth. Cut off the ends of the zip with kitchen scissors (do not use sewing scissors as the zip might damage the blades).

Turn the bag the right way out.

★ Dyeing the yarn

Dye the linen yarn as you would wool (see page 35). Prepare a cold dye bath. You can use the bath you used for the bag as it will have cooled down.

Soak the yarn. Heat for 1 minute in the microwave. Leave to dry for 10 minutes, then rinse and allow to dry.

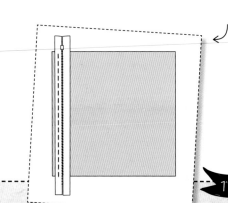

★ *Making the tassel*

Cut an 8cm (3¼in) square of cardboard and wrap the yarn around it several times. Pass a 10cm (4in) piece of yarn through the middle of the loops and knot – you will use this for attaching the tassel to the zip pull. Holding the loops carefully in place, cut the yarn at the bottom and remove the cardboard. Wrap another piece of yarn round the top quarter to create a tassel.

Knot the tassel to the zip pull.

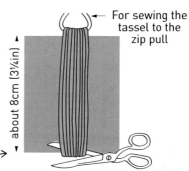

For sewing the tassel to the zip pull

about 8cm (3¼in)

Wrap the yarn around the cardboard. Pass a piece of yarn through the top of the loops. Cut through the loops at the bottom.

Tie off the top quarter of the tassel with another piece of yarn.

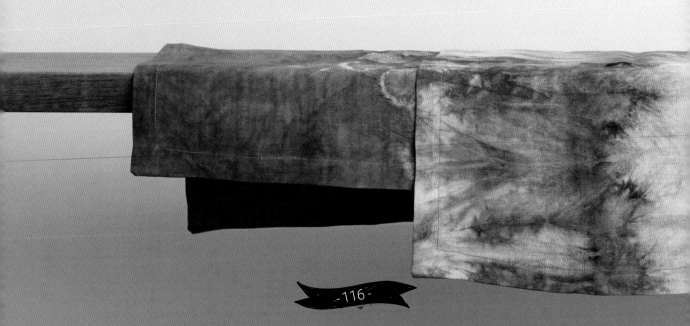

DYEING
in the microwave

CORAL DRESS
with floral corsage

EQUIPMENT

- 2.1 x 1.4m (83 x 55in) white crushed linen
- 1 spool of red thread
- 1 large safety pin
- Standard sewing box accessories

- Sewing machine
- Paper
- 1 piece of tailor's chalk or textile marker pen
- Gloves

DYE

- 1 box of coral dye (dye and fixer)
- 400g (14oz) table salt

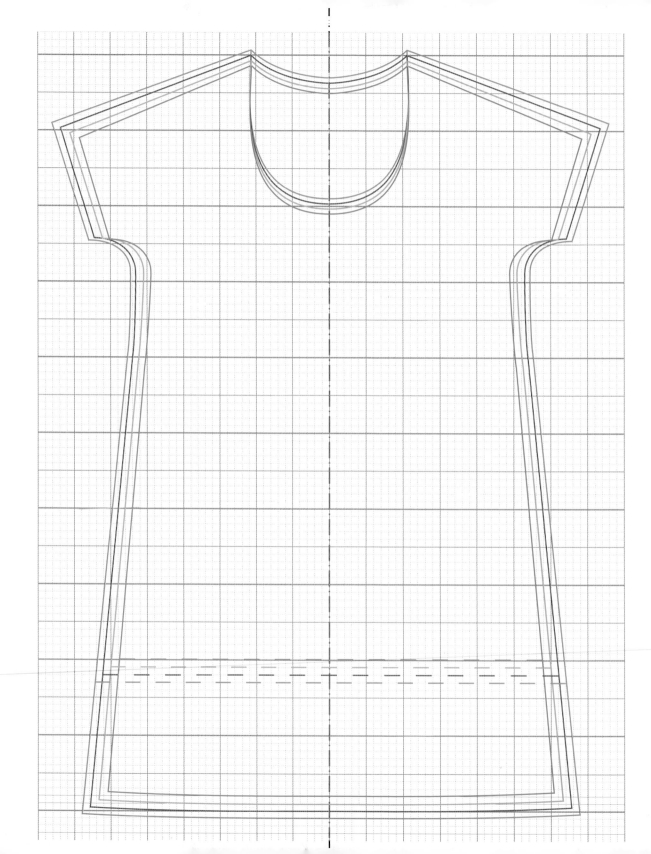

★ Dyeing the fabric

Wash the linen to get rid of any primer and to ensure that it does not shrink at a later stage.

Cut a 10 x 30cm (4 x 12in) strip of linen and put to one side.

It is advisable to dye the fabric before you make it into a dress. In a dish that fits in the microwave, prepare the dye bath with the coral dye, fixer and salt. Add 3 litres (102 US fl oz) of water. Soak the fabric in the dye bath then stir.

Put the dish in the microwave for 5 minutes on full power. Take it out and stir the dye bath.

Return to the microwave for 4 minutes. Stir again. Return to the microwave for 2 minutes.

Remove the fabric. Put aside the dye bath to use for the flower.

Rinse repeatedly until the water runs clear. Leave the fabric to dry.

★ Making the dress

Copy the pattern onto paper to real size, with the help of the grid. Add a 1cm (½in) seam allowance to the shoulders and sides, 1cm (½in) to the neck hole and 3cm (1¼in) for the hem.

Cut a front and back from the fabric, ensuring the grain of the fabric runs top to bottom on both pieces.

Place front on back, right sides together.

Stitch the shoulders together, then the sides. Oversew using a zigzag stitch.

Use zigzag stitch round the whole neckhole and the bottom of the sleeves. Turn in 1cm (½in) all round the neckhole. Iron to keep the fold.

In the same way, turn in 1cm (½in) around the bottom of the sleeves. Iron.

continued overleaf...

Seam allowances not included

1 small square = 1cm (½in)

— *UK 8/US 4*
— *UK 10/US 6*
— *UK 12/US 8*
— *UK 14/US 10*

Try the dress on to see how long you want it (in the photo it is the short version of the pattern). Mark the hem with tailor's chalk or a water-washable textile marker pen. Cut 3cm (1¼in) below. Turn up 1cm (½in) then 2cm (¾in) to the inside. Iron to keep the fold.

Set the sewing machine to the decorative stitch of your choice. Sew round the neckhole, the bottom of the sleeves and the hem in fancy stitches using the red thread.

★ Dyeing the flower

Roll up the strip of fabric. Dip the ends in the dye several times.

Put the fabric in the microwave for 2 minutes to fix the dye.

Rinse repeatedly until the water runs clear. Leave to dry.

Use the red thread and your machine to decorate one long edge of the fabric using fancy stitchwork.

Gather the strip to make a flower. Sew in place using big stitches on the underside.

Attach the flower to the dress with a safety pin.

MIX-AND-MATCH
table mat set

EQUIPMENT

- 1 old, very thick linen sheet
- 1 spool of matching thread
- Twine
- 12 small beads
- 1 roll of plastic food wrap

- Gloves
- Elastic bands
- Standard sewing box accessories
- Sewing machine

DYE

- 2 sachets of black powder dye (dye and fixer)

- 200g (7oz) table salt

★ Preparing the fabric

Cut out six 45 x 50cm (17¾ x 20in) rectangles from the sheet.

Wash them. If they are dry, first soak in water.

Prepare thcm in six different ways to give each one a different effect while staying with the same colour scheme.

★ Instructions for dyeing

To obtain a 'verdigris' look, you need to dilute two sachets of dye in 1 litre (34 US fl oz) of boiling water. Add 200g (7oz) of table salt. The thickness of the linen absorbs the dye unevenly.

Stir with a spoon or a wooden chopstick. Add a bit of boiling water, taking care not to burn yourself. Stir periodically. This may stain the areas of fabric that are not saturated a little bit. This does not matter, it is just another effect.

★ Making the first mat

Take the fabric approximately by the middle. Tie the twine round it roughly 10cm (4in) from the centre. Secure tightly, wrapping it round several times.

Dip only the centre of the rectangle in the dye container for 5 minutes. Put the dye container in the microwave for 4 minutes to fix the dye.

★ Making the second mat

Roll the second rectangle up loosely. Wrap some twine around it.

Wrap a third of the roll in plastic food wrap. Soak the remaining two thirds in the dye container for 5 minutes. Put the dye container in the microwave for 4 minutes.

★ Making the third mat

Roll up the third rectangle on the diagonal. Tie the twine around it tightly in five places. Wrap it round several times and space the twine randomly.

Soak the whole rectangle in the dye container for 5 minutes. Put the dye container in the microwave for 4 minutes to fix the dye.

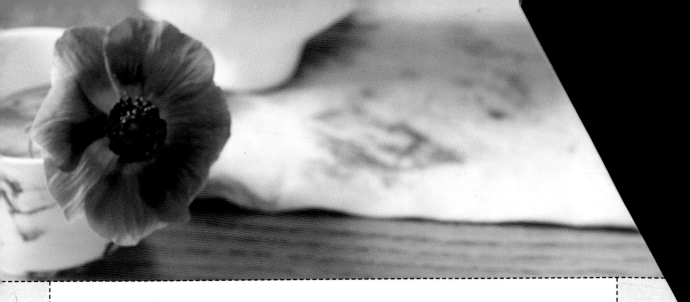

★ Making the fourth mat

Crumple up the fourth rectangle and roll it into a ball. Wrap some twine around it. Secure tightly. Soak the whole rectangle in the dye container for 5 minutes. Put the dye container in the microwave for 4 minutes.

★ Making the fifth mat

Put twelve small beads on the fifth rectangle. Knot the fabric round each of them using an elastic band. Soak it in the dye container for 5 minutes. Put the dye container in the microwave for 4 minutes.

★ Making the sixth mat

Fold the last rectangle in half. Wrap twine tightly round the middle then soak the whole thing in the dye container. Put the dye container in the microwave for 4 minutes.

★ Rinsing

Give the mats a rough rinse by hand. Then transfer them to the washing machine and run a rinse cycle. Take them out and undo the knots, removing the twine and elastic bands. Leave to dry and then iron.

★ Finishing the table mats

Turn the edges of each rectangle under 1cm (½in) and then 2cm (¾in). At this stage there is no front or back. Iron to keep the fold. Unfold. Clip the corners to make them less bulky. Refold and sew the hems on the machine.

out with the plumbing:
...e in their life!
...e of lace and her drawings;
...w to decide which colours to use.
...d Flore, who are always understanding.
...Richard for their lovely photos.

...TOGRAPHS

Thanks to Lélia for her welcome and availability.
Thanks to Zoé for her good humour.

CREDITS

Pencil pot, spotty black bag, glasses and marbled cups **Fleux**, bathroom accessories, small coffee glasses **Hema**, initialled glass **Design Letters**, ethnic patterned bowl **Jardin d'Ulysse**, teapot **Muji**, saffron glass **Ikea**, laundry basket **Landmade**, checked towel, black and white checked mug **Monoprix**, wooden Wishbone CH24 chairs by Hans Wegner **Carl Hansen and Son**, postcards **5 mai**, sandals **Kerstin Adolphson**, napkins, paper liners **Merci**.